Helping Your Anxious Child

What to Do When Worries Get Big

Julie Lowe

New
Growth
Press
WWW.NEWGROWTHPRESS.COM

New Growth Press, Greensboro, NC 27404
www.newgrowthpress.com
Copyright © 2018 by Julie Lowe

Cover Design: Faceout Books, faceoutstudio.com
Typesetting and eBook: Lisa Parnell, lparnell.com

ISBN: 978-1-948130-39-4 (Print)
ISBN: 978-1-948130-41-7 (eBook)

Library of Congress Cataloging-in-Publication Data on File

Printed in China

25 24 23 22 21 20 19 18   1 2 3 4 5

Mason is a perceptive and emotional seven-year-old boy. He reads people well, and has a particular awareness of danger and/or uncomfortable situations. Mason recently heard about a school shooting. He asks his father if it is safe to go to school; he then asks his mother if he has to ride the bus. What if someone mean gets on the bus? What if someone has a gun? Despite their comforting words, he again asks, "But how do you *know* I'll be safe?"

What can Mason's parents say to him to reassure him? What should you say to *your* children to help them with their worries and fears? How can you help them to live at peace in frightening world? How can you help them find safety in an unsafe world?

It's not only your child who is experiencing anxiety; many families are seeing an increase in anxiety in their children. With mass media and a 24/7 news cycle, kids are exposed to the reality of global perils. News of war, terrorist attacks, wildfires, Internet hoaxes, and cyberbullying spread quickly. Children and adolescents are exposed more and more to frightening possibilities of calamity. There are many other sources of childhood fear and anxiety closer to home: the flu, germs, making mistakes, getting bad grades, peer ridicule, public speaking, not fitting in, the possibility of losing a loved one—the list goes on. For kids who have a disposition toward worry and anxiety, this exposure can have a snowball effect.

Paul Foxman, in his book *The Worried Child*, asserts that anxiety is the number-one epidemic in the United States, and that approximately twenty-five percent of the population struggle with it.[1] Foxman describes how we often give children conflicting messages that the world is both safe and unsafe. We walk into public schools with metal detectors and security guards. We talk about lining backpacks with protective metals. What message might that be giving our children?

We go through airports with multiple security checks, pat-downs, and bomb-sniffing dogs, yet we regularly tell our kids they are safe and not to worry.

You've probably noticed that even though a number of children may be exposed to the same events, some struggle with anxiety more than others. Why might your child struggle more with anxiety than another child? There can be several factors. As any parent, teacher, or child counselor will tell you, every child is wired differently. They each have different strengths and weaknesses, and tendencies towards particular struggles or temptations. Some children have an innate temptation to wrestle with fear. They are more alert to potential risks and are in tune with the peril others are experiencing. This creates a heightened sense of vulnerability for them.

Some kids have personalities that are more perfectionistic, which can lead them to have difficulty relaxing, to be driven by the desire to please, to be nonassertive, and to want to avoid conflict. Kids like this often struggle with fear of people, including fear of disappointing or failing, and may put high expectations on themselves. All of these tendencies lead to stress and anxiety.

Another cause of persistent anxiety in children may be prolonged exposure to stressful situations. Traumatic events, turmoil in the family, or an unpredictable lifestyle could lead to a sense of endangerment. The more we understand the cause of a child's anxiety, the greater success we will have in shepherding him or her through it, and the wiser and more practical we will be in speaking into their experiences.

Chris is a sensitive twelve-year-old boy from a loving family. He had very few experiences of prolonged stress or loss until his grandmother passed away over the summer. Shortly after that, his grandfather also passed away, along with a family pet. Chris began worrying about his parents well-being (though they were perfectly healthy), and he became anxious about becoming ill or getting the flu. His parents became concerned when he refused to go to school one day because he knew several kids in his class had a virus. Chris's parents wondered if this was just a phase he was going through, a way of processing grief, or if he was developing a struggle that needed intervention.

As a parent, how do you know when a child's fear is within "normal" range, or when is it problematic and needs intervention? From a counseling standpoint, you'd want to evaluate to what degree it is impeding his or her day-to-day life. How frequent is the fear/anxiety, how intense is it, and how long does it last? Is it preventing your child from engaging in daily activities? Is it impeding them from taking healthy risks and engaging socially? Perhaps the better question is: Is their fear controlling them, or are they controlling their fear? Are they able to control/manage their anxiety, or does it control/manage them?

When experiencing persistent anxiety, the tendency is for children to find comfort in controlling or shrinking their world to what feels manageable. Some children look for security or comfort in routines, behaviors (such as thumb-sucking, sleeping with a parent, or other rituals), objects (escape into television, books, or fantasy worlds), people (the presence of a parent, sibling, or friend), or the avoidance of certain things (school refusal; staying home; fear of getting in a car, bus, or plane). The lure for us as adults is to try to reassure them that their fears are unfounded and that bad things won't happen. Sometimes that is the case, but most of the time, as a counselor I find that children are afraid of dangers that are genuine and possible threats.

The truth is, just like adults, children live in a fallen, broken world where bad things happen: cancer, danger, crime, and trauma are real. We all fail, make mistakes, get made fun of, and experience bullying. Life does not always turn out the way we would like it to. You will be drawn to give your children false comfort or assurances you can't deliver. Will you give in, or will you help them to navigate life in a precarious, broken world? Your hope and theirs is found in the One who reigns over it all.

Parental Comfort vs. God's Comfort

When children are hurting, most parents agree they would do anything to help provide relief. At times, this means you might settle for solutions that bring short-term reprieve but can cause secondary problems.

Take for example six-year-old Monica, who is sincerely afraid of the dark. Each night at bedtime, she begins her routine of checking under the bed and in the closet, as well as turning on night lights and closing blinds. One night, she sees something disturbing on TV. Though you've gone through her normal nighttime routine with her, she is still quite fearful. She looks panicked and is shedding tears, begging you to stay with her until she falls asleep. You've tried praying with her, playing soothing music, reading, adding a night light, and all versions of comfort you can think of. It is getting later and you all are sleep-deprived. Eventually you give in and allow Monica to settle into bed with you so you can all get a decent night's sleep. What started out as survival tool for a rough season, however, slowly becomes the new "normal." Monica likes the warmth and closeness of her parents, and battles the idea of returning to her room.

Perhaps for another child, the coping mechanism you've settled on—allowing them to watch TV until they fall asleep—has become distracting. It began as a short-term solution in a difficult moment in order to get them through a particularly challenging stretch of anxiety. Sometimes temporary decisions like these, made out of exasperation quickly become permanent habits. Kids become dependent on the TV to fall asleep, on having a parent in the room, or another less-than-ideal comfort strategy that has been put in place. Kids don't start out depending on these methods, but they can become a secondary gain to being afraid. The child starts realizing, *I get to stay up late, watch TV, sleep with my parents, or* (fill in the blank). Children might not want to overcome their fears, because it means losing something they have come to depend on or enjoy. What motivation will they have to overcome fear, if it means losing a special privilege?

Do you see how, if we are not thoughtful and careful about how we approach our children's fears, we may be unwittingly giving them reasons to maintain them?

Whatever comfort I provide my children, I hope to ultimately point them to Christ who can meet them in the midst of their fear. "Fear not, for I am with you; be not dismayed, for I am your God; I will strengthen you, I will help you, I will uphold you with my righteous right hand" (Isaiah 41:10, NKJV). As a parent, my comfort is limited; it cannot guarantee or protect them from every fear. My comfort is flawed and prone to disappoint; I will fail them, be frustrated or forgetful, or be sinful in my responses. And my comfort is not always accessible; I cannot go to school with them, live inside their head, or be available every time they struggle. However, I can point them to the One who is always accessible, always available—whose comfort is perfect and limitless.

The Spirit can go places inside a child's heart and mind that you and I cannot. I am commissioned to reflect Christ in the comfort I provide my children, always leading them to him as their ultimate comfort. He can meet them in deeper and more meaningful ways that I, as a parent, ever can, and he also desires that they learn to depend on him in all of life's situations.

Second Corinthians 1:3–4 (ESV) gives a picture of comfort that emulates Christ, "who comforts us in all our affliction, so that we may be able to comfort those who are in any affliction, with the comfort with which we ourselves are comforted by God." Here is this waterfall effect: You can provide comfort to your children because it has first been given to you. You can offer hope, because you have first found hope in him. As a parent, you live out and embody before your children what Christ is and has done for you. Kids do not need perfect parents; they need parents who walk alongside them. Children feel understood and known when they hear a parent has struggled with fear, shared their experience, and found help. They benefit by hearing how their parent found comfort in Christ, and it encourages them to draw near to God in their struggle.

God always offers his presence to his children in the midst of their fear. We see these themes in Scripture over and over:

When I am afraid, I put my trust in you (Psalm 56:3).

When anxious thoughts multiply within me, Your consolations delight my soul (Psalm 94:19, NASB).

Even though I walk through the valley of the shadow of death, I will fear no evil, for you are with me; your rod and your staff, they comfort me (Psalm 23:4, ESV).

Be strong and courageous, do not be afraid or tremble at them, for the LORD your God is the one who goes with you. He will not fail or forsake you (Deuteronomy 31:6, NASB).

Children need to find hope and comfort in the right places. We don't want to guarantee that bad things won't happen, offer false hope, or make promises we can't possibly fulfill. Young people often see through these thin attempts anyway. We *do* want to point them to the one (Christ) who can really meet them in their struggles and fears. Some kids need short-term help (accommodations, extra support, or comfort in the midst of a tragedy or hard experience); and some benefit from counseling. No matter what the severity of their struggles, all apprehensive children need to know there is a God who walks with them through their fears. Parental wisdom is knowing what type of intercession they need, while wisely, consistently pointing them to greater faith.

Giving Hope: What Message Do They Hear?

With constant media broadcasting every peril in the world, as well as more mature themes in shows that specifically target young people, the question remains: How do we infuse hope into a culture full of angst? There are many shows and miniseries out today that entice young people either with darker themes or by portraying life as meaningless. In light of the many messages children are bombarded with, there is something valuable we need to impart to them: Kids need reasons why God is relevant to them. They need to find meaning and identity in things that genuinely fulfill. They need hope.

Have we given our kids reasons why they can live life fearlessly? Have we fostered conversations about hard topics and convinced them that no topic is too touchy for us to hear, no issue is off limits, and that we can handle even the most intimate details of their lives with genuine love and concern? We must be proactive in fostering connections with our children. We must work tirelessly to engage them and invest deeply into their lives. This will powerfully counter any temptation for them to believe that what we offer is inconsequential or inadequate.

Let your child know, they are not alone. Pursue meaningful conversation with your child. Be proactive in addressing hard topics they are bound to face in their world. Be a redemptive guide speaking into the corruption they will be forced to weed through. Let them know there is One who fights on their behalf.

Thirteen Truths from Scripture to Comfort Your Anxious Child

As you foster an atmosphere of open conversation with your child, be sure to undergird your discussions with encouraging truths from Scripture. Here are some ideas to get you started.

1. You are not alone.

> Psalm 23:4: "Even though I walk through the darkest valley, I will fear no evil, for you are with me; your rod and your staff, they comfort me."

2. You have value.

> 1 Peter 2:9: "But you are a chosen people, a royal priesthood, a holy nation, God's special possession, that you may declare the praises of him who called you out of darkness into his wonderful light."

> Matthew 10:31: "So don't be afraid; you are worth more than many sparrows."

3. He sees your tears.

> Revelation 21:4 (NKJV): "And God will wipe away every tear from their eyes; there shall be no more death, nor sorrow, nor crying. There shall be no more pain, for the former things have passed away."

4. There is help.

Psalm 46:1 (ESV): "God is our refuge and strength, a very present help in trouble."

Hebrews 4:15–16 (NKJV): "For we do not have a High Priest who cannot sympathize with our weaknesses, but was in all points tempted as we are, yet without sin. Let us therefore come boldly to the throne of grace, that we may obtain mercy and find grace to help in time of need."

5. Your life has purpose.

Jeremiah 29:11 (ESV): "For I know the plans I have for you, declares the LORD, plans for welfare and not for evil, to give you a future and a hope."

6. What you are going through is temporary.

2 Corinthians 4:16–18 (ESV): "So we do not lose heart. Though our outer self is wasting away, our inner self is

being renewed day by day. For this light momentary affliction is preparing for us an eternal weight of glory beyond all comparison, as we look not to the things that are seen but to the things that are unseen. For the things that are seen are transient, but the things that are unseen are eternal."

7. There is a way out.

1 Corinthians 10:13 (ESV): "No temptation has overtaken you that is not common to man. God is faithful, and he will not let you be tempted beyond your ability, but with the temptation he will also provide the way of escape, that you may be able to endure it."

8. You are more than the outward appearance.

1 Samuel 16:7: "The LORD does not look at the things people look at. People look at the outward appearance, but the LORD looks at the heart."

9. You cannot imagine what good lies in store for you.

1 Corinthians 2:9 (NKJV): "Eye has not seen, nor ear heard, nor have entered into the heart of man the things which God has prepared for those who love Him."

10. You will not always feel this way.

2 Corinthians 4:8–9 (NKJV): "We are hard-pressed on every side, yet not crushed; we are perplexed, but not in despair; persecuted, but not forsaken; struck down, but not destroyed."

Psalm 30:5 (NKJV): "For His anger is but for a moment, His favor is for life; weeping may endure for a night, but joy comes in the morning."

11. You are greatly loved.

Jeremiah 31:3: "I have loved you with an everlasting love; I have drawn you with unfailing kindness."

Ephesians 3:17–18: "And I pray that you, being rooted and established in love, may have power . . . to grasp how wide and long and high and deep is the love of Christ."

12. You will not be put to shame.

Isaiah 54:4 (ISV): "Don't be afraid, because you won't be ashamed; don't fear shame, for you won't be humiliated—because you will forget the disgrace of your youth."

Hebrews 13:5–6 (NKJV): "Let your conduct be without covetousness; be content with such things as you have. For He Himself has said, 'I will never leave you nor forsake you.' So we may boldly say: 'The LORD is my helper; I will not fear. What can man do to me?'"

13. God is up to good in your life.

Genesis 50:20: "You intended to harm me, but God intended it for good to accomplish what is now being done, the saving of many lives."

Romans 8:28: "And we know that in all things God works for the good of those who love him, who have been called according to his purpose."

Reminding your child of unchanging promises from God's Word will give him or her a solid framework for processing worries and fears, both now and into adulthood. Because we know that God's Word does not return empty (Isaiah 55:11), we can trust the Lord to root these truths deep into his or her heart and to bring them back to mind when he or she needs them most.

Undergird all of your reassurances with reminders of who God is, who your child is in Christ, and the promises of the Lord's care and presence no matter what the circumstances are. This comfort is what your child needs most— not a promise that nothing scary or difficult will ever happen to them, but that the Lord of all creation is with them, is for them, and has a loving plan for his or her life.

Endnote

1. Paul Foxman, *The Worried Child: Recognizing Anxiety in Children and Helping Them Heal* (Alameda, CA: Hunter House Publishers, 2004), 2.

Christian Counseling & Educational Foundation

CCEF's mission is to restore Christ to
counseling and counseling to the church
by thinking biblically about the issues
of living in order to equip the church to
meet counseling-related needs.

For other resources like these,
please visit **ccef.org**

Parent by Faith at Every Stage of Your Child's Life

In this insightful parenting book, *Child Proof* explores how parents can live by faith, not formula, wisely applying biblical principles to love their children well. Julie Lowe addresses practical parenting questions and uses the CCEF model of biblical change to reveal the personal and fatherly care God has for his children.

newgrowthpress.com

Simple, Quick, Biblical
Advice on Complicated Counseling Issues for Pastors, Counselors, and Individuals

MINIBOOK
CATEGORIES

- Personal Change
- Marriage & Parenting
- Medical & Psychiatric Issues
- Women's Issues
- Singles
- Military

USE YOURSELF I GIVE TO A FRIEND I DISPLAY IN YOUR CHURCH OR MINISTRY

New Growth Press

Go to **www.newgrowthpress.com** or call **336.378.7775** to purchase individual minibooks or the entire collection. Durable acrylic display stands are also available to house the minibook collection.